Traveling Music

by Eric Greinke

Sand & Other Poems
Caged Angels
10 Michigan Poets (as Editor)
The Last Ballet
Iron Rose
Masterpiece Theater (with Brian Adam)
The Broken Lock (Selected Poems 1960-1975)
The Art Of Natural Fishing
Whole Self / Whole World - Quality Of Life In The 21st Century
Sea Dog - A Coast Guard Memoir
Selected Poems 1972-2005
The Drunken Boat & Other Poems From The French
         Of Arthur Rimbaud
Wild Strawberries

Traveling Music

Eric Greinke

PRESA :S: PRESS
ROCKFORD, MI

Copyright © 2011 Eric Greinke

ACKNOWLEDGMENTS

Most of these poems have been published or are forthcoming in the following magazines & websites: *Bogg, California Quarterly, The Chiron Review, Clark Street Review, The Delmarva Review, Edgz, Free Verse, HazMat Review, The Hurricane Review, The Iconoclast, Mad Poets Review, Main Street Rag, Modern Haiku, Muses Review, Napalm Health Spa, Nerve Cowboy, The New York Quarterly, The Pedestal, Presa, Roadrunner Haiku Journal, The Somerville News, The South Carolina Review, Tribeca Poetry Review, Under The Banana Tree & Wilderness House Literary Review.*

Kayak Lessons was published as a chapbook (Free Books, Inc., Lowell, MI, 2009).

The haiku sequences *(Shadows, Deep Moorings, Lunar Fog, The Circle Expands, Japanese Bones, Hearts Of Light)* were published in a chapbook, *Catching The Light-12 Haiku Sequences* (with John Elsberg, Cervena Barva Press, Somerville, MA, 2009).

Also, selected haiku were translated into Japanese by Ban'ya Natsuishi & published in *Ginyu* (World Haiku Association, Saitama, Japan, 2010).

Cover art by Ronnie M. Lane.

First Edition

Printed in the United States of America

ISBN: 978-0-9800081-9-7

Library of Congress Control Number: 2010908174

PRESA :S: PRESS
PO Box 792   Rockford, Michigan 49341
presapress@aol.com   www.presapress.com

Contents

4 Persona

Brief Nudity

Brief Nudity

You may glimpse it as you feel
your way to the refrigerator
at midnight or while giving
birth at 3 AM or maybe in
the damp restroom of an old
off-Broadway theater where you may
catch it revealed proudly
& professionally by a
promising younger actor.

If you happen to see it
in a good clear mirror you will most
likely focus directly
on your expressive eyes except when
your hair requires a combing
or a trim or a better color
or to be conditioned
for greater volume or thinned
to reveal or conceal you.

In The Wake

Halfway through
hurricane season,
the lost rain
returned to the body:
sad monsoon
after the big wave
that flooded
our defenseless cups,
that left us
waterlogged but thirsty,
even as the angry tide
receded,
even as the ancient tears
ran undamed
from new eyes
that opened underwater
to see the useless furniture
swirling inexorably
toward the sucking drain,
whirlpooling
with dollar bills
into a foreign currency,
faces adrift
in low vapor,
shoreline lined
with dying dreams.

Driving North

Leaving home at 6 AM,
We drive by the misty wraiths
That drift up the dreamy creek.
They settle in low places
Transforming the rising sun
Into a yellow fuzz-ball.
She multiplies & then blinds
Those who stare at her too long.

The loud crows are debating
& the seagulls are laughing
As we make our way up north,
Up the light peninsula.
The sky is a deep ocean
High above the narrow land
Where clouds float like lonely ghosts
Below the sun, our burning hope.

Shadows

Histrionic ships
Scream along the coast
Avoiding calmer waters

*

Great winds
Cross the sky
Just a play of shadows

*

Sheep
On a hillside
Wonder where to go

*

The twister touched down
On the open-palmed field
To pick up some ghosts

*

Blueberries
Grow in cedar swamps
Favored by the bears

*

Wind in my face
I beat my way home
Oak leaves go the other way

*

A stone kisses a wheel
Only to spin away
The wheel rolls on

*

Yellow maple leaves
Cover the garden beds
Fall nights wear white beards

*

Geese fly north
Against cold rain
Unaware of direction

*

Wild strawberries
Grow on low strings
Their fragrance refreshes the spirits of the dead

Dream Home

In the home of the clown there are many rooms. In the den, a statue of the Buddha palms some coins of the realm. In the bedroom, oversized clown-slippers, clown-boots & clown-flip-flops are scattered on the floor, like beached whales. There also stands the dressing table, with its oval mirror ringed with solar bulbs.

The clown looks into the mirror & sees a wise man with a big red nose.

Books line the library walls, but they are all blank except one. The music room is full of drums. The clown beats the drums to celebrate sunrise & sunset each day. The living room floor is covered with pillows & balloons of every color. Calliope music plays continuously. The clown lives tenderly alone, in his dream home.

Best Laid Plans

1.
A man planned on living.
When asked if he also planned
On dying, he replied
That dying, being automatic,
Required no planning.
"Isn't living also automatic?"
I asked him, & he said
It was time to eat something.

2.
A cowbird laid its egg
In a cardinal's nest.
It punctured the cardinal eggs
& replaced them with its own.
When the egg hatched,
The cardinals wore themselves out
Feeding the quickly growing cowbird
That they thought was their own.

Haunted Windows
for Jared Smith

Standing on sand
We peek beyond
Shafts of light
Past deeper shafts
Of darkness
We call out
Hoping to be heard
Above the rattling autos

You can see the stars
Even in the daylight
From a deep hole
This shafted wound
In mother earth
Where we were found
We cry for wings
Even as wings approach

Deep Moorings

A hard wind blows through the pines
Whispers from the past
Connect us to now

*

A kingfisher cries out
Shattering the stillness
Of the morning pond

*

A large limb falls down
Beside an old barn
Car accident down the road

*

A frog plops in a pond
Drowned-out by the sound
Of a big-rig air-horn

*

A frantic squirrel runs
Through a mad café
A door opens next door

*

Pigeons eat popcorn
In a crowded square
Falcons soar on wind currents

*

Early morning smoke
Black tar releases its heat
Road crew takes a break

*

On the evening news
Earthquakes share space
With hurricanes & tidal waves

*

The clear white moonface
Smiles above the lake
Sailboats tug at deep moorings

*

Loud television
Proffers Christmas cheer
Outside, the snow gets deeper

Traveling Music

The wounded moon
Begins its long descent.
A stable of restless horses
Whinnies in the glad wind.
Uprooted trees roam South
In search of higher ground.
We are penetrated by the water
Of the perfect rainstorm,
Leaking into the blooded ground,
Leaking into the flesh of stone
Where the hot earth's heart
Pumps mountains skyward,
To break, like waves
On salty desert plains.

One Last

Every time we passed
The old, gray barn
On our way to the lake,
We spoke glowingly
Of its stark beauty.
Inevitably,
Someone would offer
To photograph it
The next time
We came that way,
But no one ever did.
Now they've razed it.
Now, all that's left
Is a pile of ashes
On a cement foundation,
& the fieldstone silo,
Standing alone,
One last glaring erection.

Dark Star

Dark star, deadly binary nemesis
Of the transitory star we call sun,
Here we are, on beleaguered planet earth,
Worrying about our own extinction.

Dark star, parent of the next meteor,
A tsunami of lethal energy,
Serial killer of the dinosaurs,
Great reaper of scheduled massacres,
Here, we are the captives of gravity.

Dark star, our lost identical twin,
Shooting mountains in our direction,
Playing Cain to our reflective Abel,
Birthing invisible anti-matter,
Catalyst for horrific disaster.

Dark star, planetary doppelganger,
Mirror occupying negative space,
Black reflection at the vortex of time,
Here, in sunlight, we wait,

& maturate.

Lunar Fog

Man in the next booth
Complains about "Africans"
His breath smells like meat

*

He lit his cigar
Passed me a damp matchbook
With only one match left

*

A drunk woman
Stormed abuse
At her own reflection in a shop window

*

A big grey owl hears
The heartbeat of a mouse
A far cry from silence

*

Fire consumes a house
Where noone ever lived
The smoke-alarms still blare

*

Indian flutes play
Windchimes in breeze off the lake
Two ears in between

*

A '66 Beetle
Beatles on the radio
Play *Yesterday*

*

The fickle festival crowd
Checked out early
To avoid a spring rainstorm

*

A nude girl stood
Before a mirror
"*Wild Horses*" on the radio

*

Nightflowers bloom
Beneath a yellow M
Bathed in lunar fog

Metamorphosis

People of the future!
Space & time between us,
Everyone a genetic genius,
Unlike the idiots
That paddle this smoky sky.

They will wake, each day
In their pyramids & domes,
So unlike our present homes,
To play all day
With each other's clones.

They will all read poems,
Especially yours & mine,
Preserved for all time
In vast computer archives
So different from the present kind.

Wind

1.
His breathing had stopped.
A grey wind scattered the dead leaves.
Bare trees clicked their branches.
Wind bit their faces with cold teeth.
They looked with fear at the yellow clouds.

2.
"Take my hand. Let me show you
I am real." he said.

She took his hand,
& felt his breath
Filter through her body.

3.
They went out fishing.
They didn't catch a thing.

Later they went out again.
This time they filled their nets.

Wind blew over the surface
Of the cold water.

4.
When you are young
You travel where you like.

As an old man you must follow
Where you have no desire to go.

Loose Change

In an ironic twist, the man with the wooden leg kicked the shit out of the burly high school football star, with a finality born of years of patient waiting, locked & loaded, for the anticipated moment of attack.

He never knew what hit him. Was it animal or mineral? Or was it a tree, ripped from its roots, wielded as a gigantic broom? He never knew. The brain damage was swift & irreversible, the images brief.

Kayak Lessons

Kayak Lessons

1. Balance

Balance is everything in a kayak. In the wind, you must paddle harder on one side, just to go straight. Keep your nose pointed at the bow. Keep the bow pointed at your destination. Keep your back straight. Momentum will continue after you stop paddling, but the wind may turn you in a circle. You will have to get straight by digging deep, making every stroke count. In gentle water, little strokes yield big distances. In rough water, timing is the key to keeping your balance. If you lean one way, just a little, the kayak will go the opposite way. If you stop paddling, balance becomes more difficult. Better to find a rhythm that you can maintain. Direction, concentration, perception. You become the paddle, the kayak, the ocean itself.

2. How To Choose A Kayak

When you embark on a voyage in a small boat, weight is the first consideration. A buffer equal to one-half your own weight compared to a boat's weight capacity will allow you to ride high through the rough water that is sure to come.

Length is also an important consideration. Never start down a stream that is narrower than the length of your boat. Choose a boat that will take you to your destination, but also one that will allow a retreat, if necessary.

If the designer of a boat has not included a boat plug, don't buy it. If there are no bungee cords on a boat, no hatch for safety equipment & no place to rest your paddle when you need your hands, look for a boat with these features.

Don't be fooled by a high price. Focus on function, unless it's just for show.

3. The Hoody
As a surfer needs his woody, a paddler needs his hoody. Inuit kayakers wore fur hoodies, to extend the hirsute skin of the boat up, to cover the neck & the head. The kayak & the hoody go together. Never forget your hoody. The weather will change, & you can too. You can always take a hoody off, but if you forget to bring one, you may regret it.

4. Excess Baggage
In kayaking, as in life, it's better to avoid excess baggage that can weigh you down. Unless you are going into the wilderness, you don't need to pack as if you are. With baggage bungied to your bow, you will be front-heavy. When white water hits, the waves will not flow smoothly across your bow as the designer intended. Rather, they will be blocked by your baggage, which will become even heavier when soaked.

If you really feel the need to bring baggage, put it behind you, where it belongs. If you want to be buoyant, you must travel lightly.

5. Getting In & Out

Kayaks are like relationships. It's easier to get in than out. It's best to embark from shallow water, with your hull well-grounded. Hands on gunwales, carefully lower yourself into your seat. Gravity is on your side, getting in.

Getting out is trickier than getting in. As you approach the landing, you must paddle faster so you can ram the boat up on the beach, leaning back at the last moment to raise the bow. Don't fight gravity. Position your forearms on the side of the boat nearest dry land, & turn around, to kneel on the grounded hull, facing the stern. This will put gravity back on your side. Slowly stand up, all attention on balance. Take care not to trip on the cowling as you step out. This is when most people fall in the water, at the end of the trip, trying to get out.

6. Paddling

Push your paddle, don't pull it. The greatest leverage comes from the high hand, the opposing hand. You must resist the urge to pull with your dominant hand, though it may feel unnatural. After awhile, you'll get used to it. Then, you will work just as hard as before, but your strokes will be stronger. You'll go faster & further, in life & the river.

7. Fast Water

When you launch your kayak into a fast-running river, you don't have time to warm-up or practice. The power of the river catches you, & plummets you forward like relentless time.

Rocks loom in your path. You must react immediately, or you'll crash into them. Big rocks are easy to see, but submerged rocks must be identified by standing-wave, backsplash or dimple. You must read the river.

A rippled area may signify a flat rock, barely below the surface. You can surf-up on a flat rock & get stuck there. Then, the river can spin you around like a clock.

Sometimes the river spins you halfway around, then releases you, to continue downriver, backward. Then, you look at where you've been, back in time.

Going backward is dangerous, because you can't see the obstacles as you careen inevitably onward.

8. Obstacles

Obstacles can appear without warning in even the deepest, easiest streams. Watch out for submerged rocks. Watch out for low-hanging cedars with over-hanging branches. They can stab you in the face or bruise your shoulder. They can skin your forearm or capsize you. So be prepared. Bring a saw. Bring dry socks. Bring bandages. Wear a life jacket. Don't forget sunglasses. Above all, try to have fun.

9. Shallow Water

Sliding into a microcosmic world of tiny fish & underwater forests, my kayak is a floating zeppelin that eclipses the sunny beams, a giant's shadow disturbing the peace. Looking from above, I enter the minnow world briefly, but then the roar of an airplane tears me from my revery. The pilot looks down on me, then enters a cloud. A tiny turtle swims by, between the sand & the stars.

10. Spying On Wildlife
As you kayak silently down the stream, you will surprise bedded fawns, stalking herons & nesting swans. You may glide over a big gar-pike or a prehistoric paddlefish. You may see visions of tiny purple water lilies & white Japanese irises, or pass wild red roses on the riverbanks. The world takes many things.

If you are lucky, a bald eagle will swoop down to get a good look at you. Eagles often do this. They get curious when their territory is invaded & come down for a better look.

11. High Water
You see all kinds of flotsam in high water: life jackets lost overboard in the fall, sections of dock torn from shore by the last big wind, & always the styrofoam bait boxes, beer coolers & belly boards. A paddler has two options: look away at a more pristine view, or stop to clean it up.

12. Going Upstream
It takes enormous effort to travel against the stream, but sometimes you have no choice, if you have no one to pick you up at the end of your voyage. Then, you may try to paddle back to where you put in. If there are shallow rapids, you may have to leave the water altogether to walk upstream with your boat on your back.

Whenever you have a choice, always paddle upstream first, while you're still fresh. Save the downstream run for the return trip home.

13. Floating
Sometimes you will find yourself on a still pool. Don't just paddle through. This is your chance to float awhile on the thin line between the water & the sky. You can become a part of the pool's reflection, if you don't make ripples.

You never really go anywhere anyway, so why tie your craft to a delusion of destination?

Forget about your goals. Take time out to reflect, relax & restore. Save your strength for the rushing rapids.

14. The Outdoor Time Warp
Being outdoors will return you to natural time. Unlike artificial time, based on a clock, real time stretches out. (i.e. You'll think you've been outside for two hours when it's really been four.)

Fishermen, kayakers, hikers & campers know about the outdoor time warp & plan, or don't plan, accordingly. (Some wear watches to stay in touch, while others prefer to stay in touch by taking them off.)

15. Noise
No one likes a bigmouth in a kayak. A paddler needs to listen to nature. Human voices drown out the sky, the turning of the planet, the high fine galactic

symphony that is the 'music of the spheres.' Even the noisy birds can distract the listener. Even a single thought can keep you from hearing the music.

16. Reaching Your Destination

When you come to the end of your run down the river, you may feel regret that it couldn't go on longer. You may feel a strange combination of weariness & excitement. These are signs that you did it right.

If, on the other hand, you had a hard time, perhaps capsizing & getting all muddy, swearing & blaming your boat, only to complete your trip in your wet underwear, you'll be damned glad the trip is over.

Every paddler arrives at a different destination, even when everyone leaves the river at the same place.

Mild Violence

Mild Violence

A boy joins the Army Reserve
to pay for college. He gets
called up & goes
to Iraq, but afterward
his lung capacity
is that of an old man.
His sister is ashamed
to be fat, & follows
every masochistic meal
with her head in the toilet.
Some vans explode
in some cities. Thousands
are permanently poisoned
by toxic subway fumes. Our homes
are brilliant with artificial light.
Anti-bacterial hand sanitizers
kill billions of morally neutral microbes. Our
ears are blasted with the noise
of countless phones going off at once
in a crowded theater, interrupting
the entertainment.

The Vampires

Vampires have a lot
To answer for
They wear formal-wear
While they siphon the blood
From virginal peasants
Many in their own employ

They slink around
Under cover of night
Suddenly appearing
At the sides
Of their sleeping victims
Without regard to privacy

They are sensitive
To the price of silver
As well as certain commodities
Not to mention real estate
Not to mention blood banks
Butcher shops   orthodontic offices

They skip every holiday but one
They are dead on the run
Their memories are long
As are their teeth & nails
But they have no patience
Especially for the weak living

Asleep in material fortresses
Where no mirrors dare reflect
They dream of dying
Until waking to hunt
The souls of the living
Ultimate dark muggers

Who the hell are these bastards?
Why are they in charge?
The streets run red
Streams carry the blood
To the sewer arteries
To mingle with the melting sea

You might be a vampire
If you're still talking
A year after your funeral
You might be a blood sucker
If you fall asleep
To awaken in somebody's nightmare

You might be a vampire
If all the murders
Increase your profits
You might be a vampire
If everyone you see
Looks like fresh meat

This would be a good place
To live, if it wasn't
For the damned vampires
You see them lurking
Everywhere nowadays
Drinking in bars, flying on planes

Plastic surgery. Cosmetics. Vodka.
They insidiously develop land deals.
They compulsively gamble in casinos.
Their breath reeks of blood.
Their immortal souls are lost
Forever in congressional rolls.

Vultures & Vampires

When the vultures
Saw the vampires,
They were amused.

When the vampires
Saw the vultures,
They were impressed.

Each thought
That the other
Had good taste.

They all drew
Dividends
From the same account.

Some were
Fly-by-nights.
Some flew by day.

The Mutants

From the breathless moment
When they first see the light,
They are quite different.

They seem to know no guilt.
They feel no sympathy.
They just like to have fun.

They like hot, bright colors
& loud, red explosions.
They like to go too fast.

Sometimes they are damn good
At math, or even art.
Sometimes they can be smart.

But mostly they don't care,
So they plot to escape
The prison of your heart.

The Weird Wolves

There is plenty of anguished nocturnal activity in the weird wolf world. (Beastly muggings, yellow lighting, growling.)

Human by day, they stalk the canine darkness under lunar slavery, filled with carnivorous desire.

Reckless beneath the moon, they anticipate the silver bullet that will blast away the hunger that brought them out to play.

It's a mighty tough, often destructive time of life, adolescence.

The Bride

The blushing bride requires
500 lbs. of rhinestones
To be strewn lavishly
Among many thousands
Of fragrant rose petals.
She pulls a long pink train.
Her boobs are humongous
& came at a price tag
Of $6,000 each.
She sports false eyelashes
& tinted contact lenses.
Sincere tears trickle down
Her thickly powdered face,
Tracking through the glitter
On her surgically enhanced nose.
Her face is framed by a red wig
Made of hair from a real girl.

The Body Snatchers

The body snatchers work
in mysterious ways,
utilizing advanced technology.
They have full command
over the air waves
& the internet, & they
hold big shares of the dying
but strangely significant
print media. The converted have insipid smiles
& empty coal-lined eyes. If it weren't
for the underground resistance,
their dominance would be world-wide.

The Plague

Exhuming the corpses of the victims,
researchers searched for biological evidence.
They discovered deadly fleas
unlikely as black holes
that left panic in their wakes
behind merchant ships
with deadly cargoes.
The contagion became personal
through well-meaning kisses.
As always,
the rich fled to the countryside,
leaving the poor to fend for themselves.
The dead were piled everywhere,
like discarded sausages.
Religion was no comfort or respite.
Had God taken righteous vengeance?
Had they all become mass murderers?
What ancient evil drove the whales to sea?
The smell of death is difficult to disguise.
Though the penitent may scourge themselves
with whips of leather & sharp thorns,
while the innocent plead for mercy,
bloodbaths of biblical proportion
still press & flood
against our crumbling castle walls.

Persona

Persona

Coming into another spring
sixty summers down,
white light burns me
through dark days.
I peel the layers
from the onion of memory,
given the gravity of the grave.
So now my persona
is consuming my doppelganger.

I feel the triumph of stone
traveling from gravel to dust,
the fading smile
of a waning moon,
another seizure
on the seismic meter:
still one more tattoo
on the face
of my battered public bust.

Clown

I do not know me but
A train of thought
Drags me through
Illusory galaxies
Where silly circus music
Mocks my mortal wounds
While I run in circles
Wearing shoes that don't fit
An unfortunate immigrant
Buffeted by forces of history
I somehow manage
A foolish laugh
Released from myself   detached
My face a funny mask

Visitation

Walking through a broken woods,
I came upon a cottage
Which no one had called home
Since the death of an old man.
The key was easy to find,
Hidden just beneath the sill
Of the weathered front door.
As I crossed the threshold,
A hiss of "yes" echoed
From the corners of the room,
Chased by a silence so still
You could have heard a tissue
Flutter to the dusty floor.
When I walked out the door
Dust floated up & danced
To the music of the past.

The Circle Expands

We're tied to the whipping post
Chain-whipped
By the Great Chain Of Being

*

An urn of ashes
On a yellowed portrait
Paperweight of snow

*

A man enters a house
He exits sneaking out
Through a different door

*

Precarious pines
Grasp a mountain cliff
Clouds scud off to play in Maine

*

A rusty halo hangs
On an unlit taper
Out of order

*

Drunken boys drive
On crazy curves
The smell of gasoline in the air

*

The bone-handled knife
Was my favorite
I left it on a park bench

*

We will never escape
The shadows of destruction
Silence a sudden presence

*

Two tiny buttons
Saved in a box
No one knows who put them there

*

A bluegill breaks water
At the drop of a fly
The circle expands

Great Smoky Mountains

Mountains, temporal, recede
Into distant memories, mist
Seen by the surreal Magritte:
Floating rocks, hats, umbrellas
Not clouds, but green apples

Afloat, high above
The rocks that hang
Small fishes appear
From outer space, to nip
My back, an apple to bob

Bobber down, darkness
All around, a floating
Thought, gone. Below
The planets, temporarily
Disconnected, rises

A rocky garden:
My frosty breath.

Apparition

A rabid racoon stalked across the neighbor's backyard. Its eyes were milky & saliva hung like a film cocoon from its mouth. It moved slowly, back-hairs on end. When it disappeared into the woods, I was filled with horror & remorse.

The Mist

for Glenna Luschei

I wander
Through memory caverns
In search
Of the elusive present,
Like a big fish
That struggles upstream
To spawn in times river
One last time.

Like a mad wind
In an ancient storm,
Dead friends
Pierce the peaceful solitude
Where I have come
To take my soft rest
In the depth
Of a winter night's dream.

In the arid badlands
Of desire,
Past the long watches
Of sleepless nights,
I hold communion
With those lost ghosts,
Even as I pass into
The ever-darkening mist.

Cave Of The Spirits

I dreamt that the sight of the underground passages filled our hearts with an unknown light. Spirits lived in the caverns & in the giant, domed treasure room at its very center. We laughed as we entered the chamber to see the profuse silver leaves & gold apples, & the many metallic plaques, covered with stars, moons, suns & snakes. The luminous snakes were crawling up pyramids, striving for the summits, flying through the heavens with a trail of fire or lying on the reflective golden heads of the gods. The cave was deep, wide & warm. No one wanted to wake, but some of us couldn't help it.

Expressway Death

Tonight while driving out to
get my wife from a birthday party, I
saw something move 100 yards in
front of the car. A dog had just
been hit & was struggling to
get up. It looked as if its leg
was broken. I drove past on the
shoulder of the road so I wouldn't
hit it again. So did the other
drivers, although none of us
stopped to help it.

I thought about it: but maybe it
would not know me for a friend &
would bite my hand. The expressway
traffic was tedious with people
coming home after another day. I
thought: stop at the next exit
& call the humane society. I began
to feel excited over what I hoped
to do, but then I passed the exit &
kept on going. I stayed with the
traffic until my own exit.

On the way back home I wondered
if it was still there. When I saw the
lifeless shape, I recognized
my own blood staining the long road.

Japanese Bones

Dawn glows on the edge
Signaling the departure
Of the windy dead

*

Under the drum
Birch trees play timpani
In the music of the breeze

*

I crossed a windy street
To a metronome
Japanese bones ticked air

*

Spider in my doorway
Still here when I exit
Between spring rainstorms

*

A bee investigated
A rotten berry
Then hummed away

*

The cat doesn't know
That poop in a Zen garden
Ruins its feng shui

*

Rain drops on the tin roof
Footsteps hurry over
The antique covered bridge

*

A moth found shelter
From a pounding rain
Under a plastic kayak

*

Rain falls in a river
A message from the night
Kisses on wet skin

*

Light disperses from a fresh grave
Seeking out
The thirsty summer moon

Time Out

Alone on a hillside
I thought of another place
An empty field
Of tall marsh grass
In cold luxurious sunset
I saw him coming
Through the purple clouds
His hands full of stars
Released from his prison at last
While on the horizon
In a blazing mist
The light of time went out

The Way The Heat Pours Out

Your house where you keep all the lifeless birds,
Ceramic, carved in ebony, prosaic,
Silent statuettes & mobiles moving
In the window wind,
Perching on glazed branches,
Singing unheard songs.
Redwing blackbirds, purple finches & exotic
Chinese canaries
Haunt me now that the ice storms of January
Have made the air too cold for flight.
They've all gone back to Virginia now.
It's too bad we can't do that.

My house in your absence still has its dust,
Uncolored, soft as a sigh, prolific,
Lying on the window ledges & the book shelves,
Covering the paintings on the wall
With a fine kindness of distortion
Of familiar facial features.
It bothers me with its soundless sorrow,
Now that the dust has covered all
The smudges & the glass marks,
The cigarette burns & candle droppings.
All the glasses have been put away.
Dust can't penetrate a closed cupboard door.

All the birds except the songless sparrows
Have made their way back to Virginia now,
& the prolific dust has taken dominion
Over my shelves & your songless glass.
Your house where you keep all the lifeless birds,
& mine where I keep the dust,
These are shadows like the shadows on the snow
That the picket fence makes as night falls.
The songless sparrow picks & searches
Through the frost & snow for seeds,
To keep his warmth from leaving him
The way the heat pours out my door when I open it.

Refrain

Apocalyptic moments
recall scenes
of adolescent glory.
The man in the moon
transforms into
an ancient
pockmarked battlefield.
What goes up
experiences gravity,
right into the grave.

Even so, I light
my best smile
& continue to write my life,
anticipation mitigated
by anonymous regret.
Happy to be sane
underneath the sun,
although arraigned
by prosecutions of shame,
I do not refrain.

Methane

Upscale properties upstage nature.
Underground sprinkling
Competes with acid rain.
A car salesman
With a $40,000 Rolex
Searches for child pornography
On the global internet.
Above, seven turkey vultures
Spin on the thermal wind
Above the carcass of a doe.
They hone in on methane,
The familiar scent of decay.

Hearts Of Light

Deer eat magnetic trilliums
Their entrails glow above
Stars in their own heaven

*

Frosty spikes
Murderers of maternal
Stones

*

What breeze can silence light?
What sound emanates
From gasping oceans?

*

Wreathes of sunshine
Illuminate
The sandy corpses

*

Distant coyotes
Chatter hysterically
Their eyes flash like stars

*

Stars in my eyes
Centuries in transit
Fires extinguished years ago

*

The pulsating morning sun
Sings an ancient song
& we all sing along

*

Galaxies
Hearts of light
Years away

*

Exploding supernovae
Spread particles
Through droplets of water

*

Embittered light
Sees itself
In black holes

Stranded On A Cloud

A dusty statue
Of the Buddha,
Lone occupant
Of a storage unit.

Stubborn doves
Scratch in snow
Beneath
An empty feeder.

Nowhere to land
A yellow glider;
Aerial obstacles:
Flags, wires, lines.

I dwell
On my lost anchor,
Lost overboard
By my lost son.

The Accident

"Damn it, I don't care anymore! I'm getting a divorce, and that's final!" she said.

He said: "Then you'll never see the children or me alive again!" And he slammed the car door.

And then he roared off. The children were screaming in the back seat. The oak tree stood at the end of the road.

When they got to the car they saw it was wrapped like a fist on the staff of the steel-armed tree.

The children had come to earth. One was already dead. One gasped horrid breaths that wound down while they watched.

He was still in the car, his hands wrapped so tightly around the steering-wheel that they couldn't pull him away.

"Look at how his hands are grafted to the goddamned wheel." the young cop said. "Nothing could have pulled him from that wreck. Not a thing."

Final Question

If the universe
ceased to expand,
& contracted into
one last dense wish
against the dark & cold,
& the burnt-out stars
fell into
a hungry black hole,
would a memory of fire
still travel past
the catatonic stones
where light began as love
in the all conceiving night?

Cold Oceans

I sit by my open window.
A lake breeze brings the outside in.
The white pine tree makes its green stand
Between me & the foggy lake.
It grows taller with each season,
But I do not.

My height has eroded as my age increased.
Even the Rockies are half the size
Which they were a million years ago.
The wind brings the scent of the lake to me.
It blows my unsung melodies
Beyond cold oceans.

Eric Greinke, *b. 1948*, has a Master's Degree in Social Work from Grand Valley State University, in addition to undergraduate degrees in English and Psychology. He has worked in the Michigan Poets In The Schools Program, taught Creative Writing at Grand Rapids City School, and was the editor and founder of GVSU's national literary magazine *Amaranthus* (currently *The Grand Valley Review*). His poetry, essays, reviews and social criticism have been widely published in literary magazines, newspapers and online in venues such as *Home Planet News, Main Street Rag, The New York Quarterly, The Pedestal* and *The South Carolina Review*. His long poem *For The Living Dead* has received several international prizes, including *Muses Review Award* for Best Poem of 2007 and Great Britain's *Purple Patch Award* for the Best Individual Collection of 2009. His works have been translated into several languages, including French, Italian, Serbo-Croatian and Japanese. His most recent works of poetry include *Wild Strawberries* (Presa Press, MI, 2008), *Kayak Lessons* (Free Books, Inc., MI, 2009) and *Catching The Light-12 Haiku Sequences* (with John Elsberg, Cervena Barva Press, MA, 2009). He has been nominated seven times for a Pushcart Prize. www.ericgreinke.com

Also Available

Selected Poems 1972-2005
ISBN: 978-0-9740868-7-3; 140 pgs.; pp; $20.00.

"Eric Greinke's infinite variety has never staled nor withered. His poems have the surrealistic magic of Magritte or the young Dali. They awaken us with brilliant sunlight on a lake, with a rain of apple blossoms... He is an eclectic poet for all seasons and all times of the day."
-Leslie H. Whitten, columnist *The Washington Post*

"Greinke's poems are surreptitious creatures, seemingly up front at first, then grabbing hold of the reader's psyche and taking it for a ride."
-Julie Bonner Stevenson, *The Grand Rapids Press*

"Greinke seamlessly weaves together the vibrance of the naturalist with the unsettling images of dream worlds and mimes. His collection of work from more than three decades establishes him as an accomplished poet, seeing both worlds seen and unseen." -David Wheeler, *PoetsWest*

Wild Strawberries
ISBN: 978-0-9800081-1-1; 96 pgs.; pp; $15.00.

"Eric Greinke writes with a cosmological ease in Wild Strawberries *which in a breath combines the sensuality of the strawberry with the metaphysical ponderings of ghosts, spirits and zombies. Here is a clear, personal poetic testimony by an American poet that poetry is meaningful and understandable."* -David Stone, *Blackbird*

"Readers with wide-ranging tastes and free-flying imaginations may swoon over this book for its varied content and technique."
-Richard Swanson, *Free Verse*

"The true mark of art is making people think - and poet Eric Greinke does just that. Wild Strawberries *is a quick compact dose of solid, effective poetry. His variety should keep the book fresh from the front cover to the back cover. Recommended to poetry lovers everywhere and to any comprehensive poetry community library."*
-James A. Cox, *The Midwest Book Review*

Other Contemporary Poetry Titles
Available From Presa Press

John Amen
> *At the Threshold of Alchemy.* ISBN: 978-0-9800081-5-9; 86 pgs.; pp; $13.95.

Louis E. Bourgeois
> *Alice.* Chapbook; 40 pgs.; $6.00.

Kirby Congdon
> *Selected Poems & Prose Poems.* ISBN: 978-0-9772524-0-4; 84 pgs.; pp; $15.00.
>
> *God Is Dead (again).* ISBN: 978-0-9772524-2-8; 120 pgs.; pp; $20.00.

Hugh Fox
> *Blood Cocoon - Selected Poems of Connie Fox.* ISBN: 978-0-9740868-9-7; 72 pgs.; pp; $15.00.
>
> *Time & Other Poems.* Chapbook; 44 pgs.; $6.00.

Kerry Shawn Keys
> *The Burning Mirror.* ISBN: 978-0-9772524-9-7; 92 pgs.; pp; $14.95.
>
> *Book Of Beasts.* ISBN: 978-0-9800081-4-2; 64 pgs.; pp; $12.95.
>
> *Transporting, A Cloak of Rhapsodies.* ISBN: 978-0-9800081-8-0; 112 pgs.; pp; $15.95.

Arthur Winfield Knight
> *High Country.* Chapbook; 40 pgs.; $6.00.

Richard Kostelanetz
> *PO/EMS.* Chapbook; 40 pgs.; $6.00.
>
> *More Fulcra Poems.* Chapbook; 36 pgs.; $6.00.

Ronnie M. Lane
> *Morpheus Rising.* Chapbook; 40 pgs.; $6.00.

Linda Lerner
> *Living In Dangerous Times.* Chapbook; 52 pgs.; $6.00.

Donald Lev
> *Only Wings - 20 Poems of Devotion.* Chapbook; 28 pgs.; $6.00.

Lyn Lifshin
> *In Mirrors.* ISBN: 978-0-9772524-3-5; 84 pgs.; pp; $15.00.
>
> *Lost Horses.* Chapbook; 48 pgs.; $6.00.

Glenna Luschei
 Seedpods. Chapbook; 40 pgs.; $6.00.
 *Total Immersion.*ISBN: 978-0-9800081-0-4; 96 pgs.; pp; $15.00.
 Witch Dance. ISBN: 978-0-9800081-7-3 84 pgs.; pp; $13.95.
Stanley Nelson
 Pre-Socratic Points & Other New Poems. ISBN: 978-0-
  9772524-4-2; 84 pgs.; pp; $15.00.
 Limbos For Amplified Harpsichord. ISBN: 978-0-9772524-8-
  0; 144 pgs.; pp; $17.95.
 City Of The Sun. ISBN: 978-0-9800081-2-8; 126 pages, pp;
  $15.95 .
Roseanne Ritzema, (Editor)
 *Inside The Outside - An Anthology of Avant-Garde
  American Poets.* ISBN: 978-0-9772524-1-1; 304 pgs.; pp;
  $29.95.
Lynne Savitt
 The Deployment Of Love In Pineapple Twilight. Chapbook;
  48 pgs.; $6.00.
Harry Smith
 Up North. (with Eric Greinke) Chapbook; 40 pgs.; $6.00.
 Little Things. ISBN: 978-0-9800081-3-5; 78 pgs.; pp; $13.95.
Ben Tibbs
 Poems. Chapbook; 40 pgs.; $6.00.
Lloyd Van Brunt
 Delirium. Chapbook; 48 pgs.; $6.00.
A.D. Winans
 This Land Is Not My Land. Chapbook; 48 pgs.; $6.00.
 The Other Side of Broadway - Selected Poems. ISBN: 978-0-
  9772524-5-9; 132 pgs.; pp; $18.00.

**Available through Baker & Taylor,
The Book House, Coutts Information Services,
Midwest Library Services, local bookstores &
directly from the publisher -www.presapress.com**

**Exclusive European distribution through
Gazelle Book Service Ltd.
White Cross Mills, Hightown,
Lancaster, LA1 4XS, UK
sales@gazellebooks.co.uk   www.gazellebooks.co.uk**